CW01080499

THE
AWAKENING

THE
AWAKENING

ENLIGHTEN THOUGHTS

BRENDA D. HENSON

Rev. date: 07/16/2020

To order additional copies of this book, contact:
Xlibris
1-888-795-4274
www.Xlibris.com
Orders@Xlibris.com
805296

CONTENTS

ENLIGHTEN THOUGHTS

The Awakening 1

Friends.. 2

Can Anyone Hear Me? 3

I Don't Know Me 4

What You Won't Do for Money 5

Outline of Life.. 6

Dreams 7

A Woman to Be Reckoned With 8

Untitled... 9

Dreams 2 10

On the Hunt for Love 11

My Perception of Me... 13

My Sister 14

Time Is Ticking 15

Sister—Girlfriend 16

Emancipation.. 17

My Life.. 18

I See 19

I Am a Man 20

Black Man's Cry... 22

Once When He Was Young... 24

Aging... 25

When Did I Become a Bitch?... 26

Y-ME 29

I Am Fighting for My Life 31

Don't Send Me No Flowers 32

Blues Don't Live Here Anymore 33

Louisiana, That Wonderful Used to Be............................. 34

A Snowflake Falls 35

Remembrances of Fleeting Summer 36

The Rose 37

Job Don't Love Me Anymore 38

I Love You, Lord 39

God's Gift.. 40

I Hear You, Lord 41

How Can I Stop Thanking You, LORD? 42

Church Folks 43

Angels Watching, Watching over Me................................... 44

God Is... 45

God Is Watching over Me 46

Heavenly Hands 48

I Wish I Could Fly... 49

God's Child 50

THOUGHTS OF LOVE

Love Comes Again.. 53

My Husband, My Man, My Life 54

This Time It's for Real 55

I'm Getting Ready for My Man to Come Home 56

'Cause I Wont's Me a Man... 57

Remember Me.. 58

Dark Days 59

If You Let Me... 60

The Familiarity of You... 61

May-September Affair 62

Let Me Love You 63

Telephone Love 64

Just for the Love of You 66

An Unconditional Love.. 67

The Essence of You.. 68

When Did You Know You Loved Me? 69

You Are My Beloved 70

You Look So Finger-Lickin' Good 71

Eyes—the Mirror of Your Mind 72

Love Left Me 73

Close to You 74

Runaway Love 75

I Love You, Girl 76

The Cheating Kind 77

The First Time I Made Love 78

I Miss You 79

Took Me Out 80

HOW DO I MAKE LOVE

My Sadness Cry 83

Jay 84

Death Has No Restrictions! 85

I'm Mad 86

Katrina's Destruction 87

Escape 89

Sadness Go Away 90

OTHER POEMS

The Weighting Game 93

Jimmy 94

Pinky 95

Penny Luck 96

Party 97

Aunt tee tee 98

Ugly Thang 99

Oprah 100

Family Reunion 101

The New Year Promise 102

Sleep of Wondrous Sleep 103

Mandingo Man.. 104

Excitement..105

Richard, I Miss You Already 106

Christmas Cheer 107

I Love Shoes.. 108

Shopping Addiction... 109

Sleepwalker 110

Good Old Nurses.. 111

Mister Cool 112

Badonk-a-donk Butt..113

Talking Chatty Cathy 114

Chocolate Jones...115

Sophisticated Lady 116

Black Girl 117

My Son 118

A Love Poem to My Granddaughters 119

The Country Preacher 120

Puerto Rican Girl 121

Bruce the Barber 122

Jazz Man 123

I Love You, Daddy 124

Dear Mama 125

Peace Be Still 126

So Easy and So Cheap 127

Displaced African Queen................................... 128

Closet Fast Girl... 129

Crazy Girl Friend 130

Pretty Brown Horse Man 131

Unbelievable Drama Queen 132

Big-Boneded Baby 133

To My Daughter 134

Sha'Quaan 135

Big Ole Fat Girl...136

About the Author..137

About the Book 139

Enlighten Thoughts

The Awakening

How long have I known?

Why was it shown?

Awaken from this dark and sightless path—

Fallen prey to the obscurity of vision—

Suddenly blinded by the light.

Friends

Having mirrors of my mind with like images.

Going through life at an uneven and awkward pace.

Unsure of life's challenges and disappointments.

*Wading in a sea of uncertainty with you
constantly reassuringly by my side.*

Can Anyone Hear Me?

I am screaming in silence in this dark cavern of light.

I am walking noiselessly in this stampede of confusion.

I am crying without tears in this sea of hopelessness.

I am whirling on the tabletops in a legless community.

I am calling out loud in a voice of vast anticipation.

I am this beautiful flower in a bed of despair.

Can—anyone—hear—me?

I Don't Know Me

I show my love to my love unabashed.

I hid myself from myself to let no one in.

I sacrifice my experiences to a memory fading slowly.

I explore my inner self and am afraid to reveal it to you.

Calmly I talk and rapidly I deteriorate
into - and self-destruction.

Come, rescue me from myself before I am lost in myself.

What You Won't Do for Money

A pretty girl standing aimlessly on the corner looking for love,

A mother of five with no job and a physically abusive husband,

A lawyer's justification for defending the guilty murderer,

*A child abused, praying for an end to this
nightly game for lunch money,*

And

Me—

*Working that nine-to-five, forever
running and getting nowhere.*

Outline of Life

Darkness falls with suddenness.

Quiet comes silently.

Trouble comes in abundance.

Prosperity is unexpected and new.

Learning is all about what you want.

Heartache is a condition of life.

Understanding is an individual affair.

Love comes and goes without urging.

Hate is and is not expected.

Compassion is provided in increments.

Pain is always unwelcome.

Life is learned over and over again.

Death is final.

Dreams

I DREAM OF,

Walking on the rainbows of a child's imagination,

Youth and wisdom simultaneously,

Holding hands with you till the twilight of life,

Life's drama unfolding immaculately,

Sweet love unconditional and pure,

You.

A Woman to Be Reckoned With

I am Angela Davis, Oprah Winfrey, and Maya Angelou.

I am a woman to be reckoned with. How 'bout you?

Breaking from this cascade of uncontrollable apathy,

Giving homage to my predetermined destiny,

Providing for the world, I am a lady-in-waiting.

Soon Prince Charming will come along
and set my heart pacing.

Almost struck down in the prime of life
by an unforeseen condition

Only to rise again by her own volition;

Give God the glory, for in Him all miracles lay.

And in the end, that only is what will keep the devil at bay.

Pray and praise Him; Pray and praise Him
every day in order to make it in

God's way.

Untitled

Love me

        Like the newborn loves its mother.

Caress me

        Like the waves caress the shore.

Adore me

        Like a man adores his wife.

Console me

        Like you mean it.

Protect me

        Like a mother bear protects her cub.

Honor me

        Like the child honors the elders.

Pray for me

        Like Jesus prayed for our souls.

Dreams 2

Dreams are the essence of one's unfulfilled reality.

They vaporize with the kiss of the morning sun.

Easily remembered are the horrific ones that shock the soul;

*Fleeting are the warm and fuzzy ones you
embrace for the sake of sleep.*

Take care not to let your dreams control your life.

Keep them as a respite from the trials and turmoil of the day.

*Never become part of the dream's desirable
unrealities or become permanently*

lost in your mind.

On the Hunt for Love

Feel me with your eyes
                    closed tight.

Touch me with your open heart
                    full of love and desire.

Love me unconditionally with overwhelming passion
                    overflowing.

Claim my soul as though you owned it from
                    a past life.

Kiss these lips with your lips, deep, succulently, soulfully, with
the heat of a hundred
                    sunrays.

Hold me in your arms like it is the last time
                    forever.

My eyes are dimmed from the light of
                    lost love.

Gravity no longer holds me as I flail aimlessly through life in
this unending atmosphere
                    of sadness.

I crouch and pounce, delving into one lovesick disaster
                    after another.

Returning home love drunk, sick, and disgusted from a sloppy and uneventful

affair.

Shrieking cries of the aftermath haunting me day after day with no relief.

Insanely starting the hunt all over again and falling once again in that love lost

trap.

My Perception of Me

I am ugly, so you say, in appearance, and you treat me as such—
But my soul is beautiful

I am sad, and you treat me as such—
But my being secretly exudes happy, and yet I am shy and
Cannot show you my other side for fear of disappointment and
rejection.

I am depressed, and you treat me as such—
But my depression is a façade to keep the enemies inside my
head
At bay, to protect me from the world who would use me, reject
me, and
Prostitute my energy or lack thereof for their own individual,
selfish gains;
Tired, tired of being in this frame of mind and spirit.

So,
I dress myself up, dress my face up, dress my hair up, and
change my attitude and leave your sorry ass.

I look in the mirror and see a
Beautiful, peaceful, secure, self-assured, unabashed, happy
individual.

I will not go back; I will not falter; I will never sacrifice the love
of me for the love of you—

Never, forever.

My Sister

*Sisters cut from the same cloth, answering my
unspoken questions with not as much as a mutter.*

*She knows my thoughts as well as her own; we were
both present when our thoughts were grown.*

*She loves me; she hates me; it's a day-to-day affair, and
she can suck information from me like a vampire.*

*I miss her when I am away from her; she is my very best
friend, and the love-hate relationship will exist till the end.*

*My sister, my treasure, my one of a kind—would
not trade her for the world. We are aligned.*

Time Is Ticking

*Time is an important commodity that
is not to be wasted: ticktock.*

*When you are young and innocent, there's
plenty of it; you got ticktock.*

*In your youth, there is plenty to spare, but
it's wasted every day: ticktock.*

*Seconds, minutes, days, months, and years
speed by before you know it: ticktock.*

*You look around, and with no rebound your
time is drawing near: ticktock.*

*Hold precious to your valuable time; no one
all else will consider it as such: ticktock.*

*Let nothing or no one steal your valuable
time; all added up, you could miss a lot
of time: ticktock. ticktock, ticktock, ticktock.*

Sister—Girlfriend

My sister, that's what I call her. She's been so
close it would be difficult not seeing her.

I've known her for years; she knows all my thoughts and
plans and stamps her voice of approval like Queen Anne.

A call or visit is always welcome; she knows
this with never a word mentioned.

Children and grandchildren we've had, and
friends we remain—true sisters to the end,
This we maintain:

Though miles separate us, the phone lines are abuzz—
keeping Illinois Bell in business is not our plaything.

To the end she will be my sister—girlfriend—
this to some others' chagrin.

Emancipation

I am seeing light-years of possibilities
dwindle before my very eyes—

The explosion of grief in
bright, brilliant colors,

The anticipation of despair, dried
up like a raisin in the sun.

Walking through life in a depressed state,
confused with blinders on,

I am seeing love evaporate like
yesterday's rainclouds,

While the awaking on the human side
is justified and full of dance.

My Life

I lived in fear of the gangs who were
like pests that permeated the concrete community.

I walked through neighborhoods with sidewalks
littered with old used syringes and crack pipes.

I passed the whores on the corner watching me off to
school as they solicit the johns that frequent the hood.

I watched my father beat my mother out of frustration, after
working days of double shifts just to make ends meet.

You are a product of your environment, or so it's said.

I reminisce about my past as I sit in my office, viewing my
MD Credentials, waiting to attend my
patients—all in a day's work.

I See

I see water lilies floating on a still pond,
Glassily reflecting themselves in themselves.

I see horses running across a wide-open grassy plain
Running so fast, giving the appearance of
being still in flight in the distance.

I see birds in flight, gliding gracefully in and out of the clouds,
Giving the appearance of sky dancing.

I see trees lined on the forest edge,
Looking as if God drew them with His mighty hand.

I see you of God, made from God, with the love of God—
His son,
Jesus.

I Am a Man

Not a baby daddy,

I court my lady and respectfully
ask her parents for hand in marriage—
that is the grand plan.

I party in the lounges all night
and sleep all day with the first
available lady—don't tie me down.

We get married, have children, go to
church and pray together, raising
our children in a spiritual, educational,
and respectful environment.

She got pregnant on her own. I had
nothing to do with it. She should
have been more careful. How do I
know the kid is mine?

Our children grow up in a warm, nurturing
environment, become educated and
celebrated, and carry on the family legacy.

Child grew up never really knowing
his father or mother, feeling abandoned
by a nonexistent father and a mother
working day and night, staying home alone.

Now ready to carry on the tradition taught
by good and loving parents and to pass on
to future generations love, honesty, respect,
and the love of God.

Now ready to pass on to future
generations distrust, anger, disrespect,
and never knowing God.

What is your choice:
to be
a man or a baby
daddy?
The choice is up to you.

Black Man's Cry

Mother

Didn't I show appreciation for the love you gave me?
Stop sweating me!

Father

Didn't I become a man just like you taught me?
Stop sweating me!

Teacher

Didn't I go to school and learn the golden rule?
Stop sweating me!

Boss

Didn't I work from 9-9 and didn't get paid an extra dime?
Stop sweating me!

Wife

Didn't I make sweet love to you on Friday, and heard you
scream 'til Sunday?
Stop sweating me!

Children

Didn't I care for you with love and understanding?
Stop sweating me!

Friend

Didn't I support you, when others turned their backs on you?
Stop sweating me!

Preacher

Didn't I go to church on Sunday and tithe unfailingly?
Stop sweating me!

Collectors

Didn't I pay my bill on time?
Stop sweating me!

World

Didn't I justify my existence in my ways and deeds to society?
Stop sweating me!

Once When He Was Young

*There he lies old, gray, and weak, a mere shadow of
the tall, strong, strapping, young man he used to be.*

*He walked the beaches in his swimming trunks muscles
glistening in the summer sun, laughter in his eyes and face as
the other sun worshipers admired his tall, muscular frame;
he was young; he was strong; he had his life before him.*

*He ran and jumped, he swam until he felt that his
heart would burst, rest and swim once more. He was
young; he was strong and full of ambition and love.*

*Now he lies in his bed weak and restrained by
age and the physical circumstance of life, which
brings on age and tired before you know it.*

*Time flies when you are having fun, but it goes
by just as quickly when your end has come.*

*He lies in bed feeble and tired from life's pleasures and
treasure, trials and tribulations. If asked about his life's
adventures, his answer is he would not change a thing.*

*Now all he has time to do is reminisce and go over his life's
events in his mind—a mind that comes and goes from time to
time—and he thinks about the time when once he was young.*

Aging

As I look into the mirror, my mother's face I see.
When did this happen right in front of me?

I use creams and potions day and night,
which remain discreetly out of sight.

Fine line and wrinkles quickly appear,
and now gray hair is everywhere.

The moles I thought are aging spots,
and now I can play connect the dots.

Knees creak and cry when I stand up.
My grandchild says, "Grandma, you cracking nuts?"

My get up and go has gone over yonder.
Should I try Ginkgo? I ponder.

Whoa is me. What can I do?
The aging process is not through.

It's harder to remember when I was young and fertile;
now I just want a good-fitting girdle.

Life passes quickly like the snap of a finger,
so don't be in life a constant malinger.

Wake up and smell the roses, and don't let life pass you by.
Aging is God's way of telling you your time is drawing nigh.

When Did I Become a Bitch?

In old poetry, prose, song lyrics, and such,
I was, My lady, sweetheart, lover, and friend.

Tell me, "When did I become a bitch?"

Webster describes a bitch as a "female dog, wolf, or fox etc.,
etc., so on and so on."

When did we denigrate our character to that level of low? We
have so very far to go.
Father used to respect us, brothers used to accept us, boyfriends
and husbands used to love us when did we miss the bus.

As your mother, I carried you—for nine months nurtured you
in my womb. You fed from me nutritiously; wholesomeness was
provided you. Let no harm come to you and introduced you to
the world.

I grew you up, schooled you, taught you and learned you,
provided and protected you, raised you to be a respectful,
healthy, and well-adjusted Black man.

Tell me, "When did I become a bitch?"

A grandmother's love is a fierce and special love, filled with
hugs and kisses. Set you on my knee, loved and protected you
unrequitedly, would die for you, cried for you at you birth,
graduation, and marriage.

Tell me, "When did I become a bitch?"

I am your sister; we fought and went to school together. You were my big/little brother— defended you to the death against any kinds of threats, lied for you, cried for you, and took too many whippings for you.

Tell me, "When did I become a bitch?"

You are my uncle; I am your niece, walked proudly by you side. My friends thought you were sooo fine, and I pretended you were mine all mine. You defended me and pretended to me that I was all that cute. Shoot.

"Tell me, when did I become a bitch?"

Now you are what you are not because of your life's events but because of currents trends. Can we turn back the clock? Can we start from the beginning? Let's reevaluate, re-determine and find out what we did wrong. Society said you were worthless; raised nevertheless to be a respected man.

Was I too accepting, not objecting, leading to this state and situation? Look life over. Let's get closer and make some drastic changes in this female/male exchange. It would be amazing if the mudslinging could come to a final halt.

And

Respect me forever in the now and ever, and stop calling me that dreaded name "bitch."
It would be better for our sons and daughters to stop and switch.

So I ask you, beg you, request and implore you to stop using that dreaded name—bitch.

Y-ME

Woke up this morning
Not a care in sight.

Showered, shaved, and dressed
Looking forward to the day's delight.

Routine breast exam performed
Without fear; a lump I did feel, which
Brought me to tears.

I have been so careful—eat right, and
Exercise y-me is my refrain; this is
Totally unjustified.

My doctor set me up with the usual tests;
Surgery, next x-ray, then chemo the real
Treat.

I survived it all through persistence and
Prayer to live another day to survive, to strive,
To make life better in every way.

Breast cancer a dreaded disease to beat,
Yet survive to encourage each other to
stay alive, is a family treat.

Remember, God loves you and so do we.
Stay focused and know that you will live
To fight this disease.

To Verlie with love

I Am Fighting for My Life

I am running through gang-filled neighborhoods,
walking on streets littered with drug paraphernalia
to try to get to school.

I am walk on a balance beam daily over sky rises,
risking life hundreds of feet in the air to feed
my family.

I am working deep underground in dark caverns,
Inhaling coal dust to put a decent
meal on my table.

I am dangling on the sides of high-rise buildings
keeping the windows clean and neat to
put my kids through college.

I am patrolling the streets both day and night,
star on my chest, gun holstered at my side to keep
the streets a safer place.

I am entering burning buildings with water and hose
saving lives, only to jeopardize my own.

I am a victim of an incurable disease seeking
and searching for a permanent or temporary cure,
to
      continue
          to
               enjoy
                    life's
                         pleasures.

Don't Send Me No Flowers

Don't send me no flowers not after I'm gone,
Can't smell them long after I'm gone.

Give me flowers while I'm alive and ticking,
I want to see them, smell them while
my well-sprung is kicking.

They load up your casket and your grave overabundant;
I would rather see them, smell them in a -pitcher, bowl
Or at a beautiful shore front planted,

So I say to you all, all who don't know, celebrate with
Flowers for birthdays, anniversaries
with huge bouquets in tow.

Blues Don't Live Here Anymore

The black clouds lifted, what do I see? A
bright, clear world all around me.

Darkness and despair won't last forever,
but while here it must seem an
overwhelming endeavor.

The sun shining so sunny and bright, dark
days gone, no blight in sight.

How could I have fallen into those dark
days of despair, feeling so low and
foreboding with no one to share?

Always reach out to those in need; your
time may be next as sure your life
proceeds.

It's never too late—look, watch, and listen.
Blues is a fate we all want to be missing.

Louisiana, That Wonderful Used to Be

Bourbon Street, French Quarter—that twenty-four-
hour ground—no one had a bad time when
it was around.

No longer there—filled with water everywhere—
will it reopen is everyone's care.

Party, party, party was the order of the day;
now that it's gone nowhere can take
its place.

Reopen, repair is the order of this day—
rising from the ashes and the decay.

New Orleans, Louisiana, will never be the
same; maybe it will be better rising from
the flood and flames.

A Snowflake Falls

*I gaze out my window and see the snowflakes fall so graceful
and crystal blue.*

They sparkle like silver under the light of the moon.

*It piles so high yet so beautiful and cold; brave this
unprepared, and you will not have to be twice told.*

*It's been said no two are alike, so who's been counting? If he
comes forth, what is his method and accounting?*

*Snowflakes a creation from God above—
his creation made for us
to observe and love.*

Remembrances of Fleeting Summer

Soft winds blowing across my face,

Beautiful beds of flowers blooming everywhere,

Emerald green beds of grass soft and alluring,

Multicolored green leafy trees swaying in the breeze,

Soft white billowy clouds overhead with a blue sky backdrop,

Beautiful golden sandy beaches with bathing-
suited bodies dotting the shore,

Children playing on the monkey bars—
gales of laughter for all to hear—

Lovers strolling hand in hand in the
parks stealing kisses after dark.

Alas, summer is over, and fall, then winter begins.

The Rose

This flower blooms each day at noon, such
a beautiful flower I wait for the hour.

Its glorious opening is such a joy, I wait with
bated breath for the bloom to deploy.

Its petals are perfectly edged in pale pink
all else white, the beauty of God's
creation to enlighten our life.

Given as gifts and well received by all, who
could resist when they make their call?

So lovely to look at and anxiously received,
a rose when given can never be
misconceived.

Roses are given as singles, bunches, or dozens;
however received can always be
considered a blessing.

Job Don't Love Me Anymore

I go to work most every day and work so
hard to get a good day's pay.

I try to do the best I can, but the boss
won't give me a second chance.

The world is filled with insecure folks, who
work at being your number one foe.

I work hard all day and give all that I'm able,
and at the end of the day I feel my
job unstable.

I took the job full of ambition and spunk;
reports are getting back that you think
my work is pure junk.

It's hard for me to understand why you
have perpetuated this scam.

Be damned if I don't, be damned if I do, there
is no pleasing you. At the end of
the day I might as well say ... I'm through.

I Love You, Lord

I love you, Lord. I love you, Lord. I Love you, Lord,
Yesterday, today, and tomorrow.

You opened up my eyes and gave me a different sight.

You opened up my heart and gave me a different start.
I love you, Lord, yesterday, today, and tomorrow.

I love you, Lord. I love you, Lord. I love you, Lord,
Yesterday, today, and tomorrow.

I was once full of sin until you took me in. I love you, Lord,
Yesterday, today and tomorrow.

You opened up the door, and I have sinned no more.
I love you, Lord, yesterday, today, and tomorrow.

And I say, I love you, Lord; I love you, Lord; I love you, Lord,
Yesterday, today, and tomorrow.

Your loving grace took me out of the rat race.

My life has been changed; it will never be the same, and I say,
I love you, Lord yesterday, today, and tomorrow.

I love you, Lord. I love you, Lord. I love you, Lord,
More yesterday, today, and tomorrow.

God's Gift

I behold the brilliance of the setting sun—
an enormous yellow-orange ball
On the backdrop of the blue gray sky.

Seeing the sky meet the ocean and the
appearance of the sun dipping
Into the ocean is a sight that can only be
described by the Seeing Eye.

What a pleasure it is to see such a magnificent
God-given glory magnificent
And free for all to see.

The best things in life are free, and
this is yours for the viewing.

I Hear You, Lord

You gave me my mother, who protected me by day and night;

You gave me my Father, who worked tirelessly for his family rights.

Church on Sunday to learn right from wrong,

Pray and praise him in between to keep my spirit strong.

Work imprinted on how to live my life,

And whispers from you, dear Lord, to remind me and keep me right.

Out of habit I would stray away, but your love brought me back home to you each and every day.

I will never lose sight of my perfect heavenly home no matter where I roam.

One day I will be called to be in that number,

And my time here on earth I won't have to wonder.

Keep the Lord's name on your lips and in your mind;

When it's all said and done, only he has love unconditional and divine.

How Can I Stop Thanking You, LORD?

You gave me loving parents, who were not afraid to show me love and affection.

You gave me life unconditional so profound and unexpected.

You gave me my family that I cherished every day.

You gave me my child, and my love grows for her day by day.

You gave me my grandchildren—the ultimate joy of my life.

You gave me happiness that I try to share with others in my life walk.

I am grateful for all you give and do for me, but most of all, dear Lord, I love that you gave me You!

Church Folks

I go to church, fall down on my knees and
pray, please Lord forgive me of my sins
this day.

The church is filled with lost souls and
sinners, coming to church to get
strengthened,

Church folks are a different breed; they will
pray for your soul at length indeed.

The world is filled with sin-filled people, who
need to be in church—the important
cathedral.

Some are saved, sanctified, glorified, and
filled with the Holy Spirit; they feel
prayers are only answered when done with great reverence.

To guide your way to heaven, thank the Lord
every day, and you will receive your
blessings in every way.

Angels Watching, Watching over Me

Angels watching over me by day and night.

*When the storms are rising, and the dark
clouds are forming, I know that the
angels are watching over me.*

*When the devil's advocates come from all
over forming a circle around me, the
angels are watching over me.*

*When they talk about me and persecute me, the
angels are watching over me.*

*When Mama and Daddy and siblings put me down, the
angels are watching over me.*

*When friends scorn me and treat me lowdown, the
angels are watching over me.*

*The angels watching over me by day, angels
watching over me by night, angels
watching clearly out of sight.*

*Victory is mine; victory is mine, because the
angels are watching over me, my Lord.*

God Is

God is:

In the trees, grass, flowers, and in the leaves,

In a baby's smile at seeing its mother face again and again,

In the miracle of life as it begins and troubled times when it ends,

In early worship services on Christmas morning at ten,

In love shared by all in the human race with no exceptions based on time or space,

In the warmth and love of an unsolicited embrace,

In the light summer breeze across my face, and

In the blessing of the sun and stars across the sky, just in case.

God Is Watching over Me

*I wake up in the morning being gently
awakened by the sun's warm rays, eat
breakfast, meditate, and contemplate God's good grace,*

*Get dressed and go safely having nothing
to fear, going on my way toward my
career,*

'Cause God is watching over me.

*I go to work and make it through the day;
no anger or guilt will influence my
pathway;*

*I work so hard for the money I'm paid, to
earn an honest and daily wage,*

'Cause God is watching over me.

*Take care of my kids, my husband, and my
house; without God's blessing I would
have none, no doubt.*

*The world is filled with thankless people, not
knowing that God should be at the
top of their steeple.*

I don't take for granted life's ever-changing
demands, and I would not want to
exist without His commands,

'Cause God is watching over me.

Heavenly Hands

Heavenly hands woke me up this morning
and guided me on my way.

Heavenly hands keep me and protect me,
watching over me day by day.

Heavenly hands direct me, keeping me out of harm's way.

Heavenly hands, heavenly hands, heavenly hands.

Heavenly hands have been closer than
any earthly friend of mine.

Heavenly hands told the devil she's not yours; she is mine.

Heavenly hands they rest on me, calm my spirit, can't you see?

Heavenly hands, heavenly hands, heavenly hands.

I Wish I Could Fly

Like a bird in the sky, soaring on high,

Dipping in and out of the mountains and crevasses with ease,

Lightly skimming the water, and feeling
the spray across my face,

Gliding with the wind softly, gently
caressing beneath my wings,

Enveloped in the current, taking me ever
higher above the soft billowy clouds,

Eyes closed wind blowing against my face
lightly like tiny fingers across my skin,

Wind going through my hair ticklingly,
causing neck hairs to stand on end,

Landing ever so softly on wind-bent grass
as if made into a cushion just for me,

I lay and watch the clouds slowly drifting
by, Oh! How I wish I could fly.

God's Child

I am God's child, and this I know,
for He speaks to me and guides me everywhere I go.

Sometimes my way is rocky, and sometimes it's smooth,
but He is always with me no matter the road I choose.

Life was not promised to be easy,
although at times I wish it wasn't so rough.

As long as I know that God has my back,
life's problems will not be too tough.

Thoughts of Love

Love Comes Again

It's about time I met you.

You have been so out of reach.

My heart is encased in years of disappointments,
Waiting for that proper release.

We met on a Sunday; by Friday we were in love.

Saturday we were married and swooning like two doves,
So come on, love take over.

The wait is long overdue,
And this time that I've got you, I promise it will be true blue.

My Husband, My Man, My Life

As I gaze at the picture of your face so strong and true, I think about our life.

*I am mesmerized thinking about the way you walk, the way you talk, and your
brilliant smile.*

*With my eyes closed, my heart melts when I visualize you playing with our child,
knowing that this type of attitude is not in style.*

*You promised me a life of happiness and adoration, which remained true despite
life's aggravations.*

*On a bright, sunny day, a car crash took you away from me, and no one can ever replace that indomitable spirit of my husband, my man, my
life.*

This Time It's for Real

Yo mama had you, but I got you now. I wake up in the morning thinking about yo
fine ass.

What we gonna do to make this love last?

Trials and tribulations don't last forever, but it seems like an eternity since we been
together.

I fell to my knees last night and prayed to the Lord above.

Please send me back your original love.

Gone forever out of my life, can I take back the things that I've done?

I promise, please, baby, please come back to me.

And I will show you what real love can be.

Because this time it's for real!

I'm Getting Ready for My Man to Come Home

I wait all day cause he works so hard;
his daily grind keeps him out till the dark.

He calls and checks in and finds me hard at work;
cleaning the house, making the beds to please
him is as automatic as clockwork.

Dinner prepared—his favorite meals—it's what
he loves; it's no big deal.
The bath is drawn—his scented odors—waters warm
and aids in the day's healing and others.

My body warm and prepared for love,
we will cuddle—snuggle all night like two hungry doves.

The night passes; the day is dawning, and I'll start
all over. My daily routine won't be undercover,
'cause I'm getting ready for my man to come home.

'Cause I Wont's Me a Man

I cut my hair and put on a wig, 'cause I wonts me a man.

I eat all day and work out all night, 'cause I wonts me a man.

I wear beautiful lingerie and baggy blue jeans
and sweatshirts on top, 'cause I wonts
me a man.

I give myself a facial every day and put on
expensive creams; cover it all with large hats
pulled down over my face, 'cause I wonts me a man.

I learn all the poetic prose and love songs by
the score, and can never give anyone a
kind word, 'cause I wonts me a man.

I go to the popular clubs and stand around with
an evil look on my mug, 'cause I wonts
me a man.

I go to the best school and learn perfect English,
yet choose to only speak in ghetto
slang, 'cause I wonts me a man.

I stay at home wondering why I am the way I
am, 'cause I really, really, really wonts
me a man.

Remember Me

How will you remember me? Will you remember
the times I had to whip that butt,

Or

Will you remember the hugs and kisses
as I read you to sleep at night?

Will you remember the lessons I made you
learn and learn by trial and error?

Or

Will you remember our loving talks with teasing laughter?

Will you remember the long, loving glances
I gave you when my heart was so
proud it would burst.

Or

Will you remember the overpowering anger
that seemed to last forever and a
day?

Will you remember the good times, the happy times
we shared together?

Tell me,

How will you remember me?

Dark Days

Dark days don't seem so dark when I'm with you.

Dark clouds look sunny and bright when I'm not feeling blue.

You made my long days short and sweet
and my life so complete. If I
lose you, what will I do?

Our life conjoined, and I haven't felt better;
it's been eons since my life has
had such pleasure.

It's been a long time since I've felt like this—
forgotten what love was like—
but memories all flood back, and I'm back
on track, and I'm flying higher
than a kite.

I look forward to the intimate call and get-togethers with such
anticipation, and being near you to hear
you satisfies me and gives me
inspiration.

Time appears to stand still when I wait
for you to come, but soon the
wait is over, and all my desires are resumed.

Unlucky in love, unlucky in life until I met
you; a new lease is earned, and
I will be damned if I turn away from this love returned.

If You Let Me

Hey, baby, I know what you need. I'm
gonna wine you and dine you and
knock you to your knees.

All you have to do is turn off the light,
and light the candles cause I'm
gonna give you what you need.

Have you been thinking about me? I
know you have because I put
something on your mind that can't be erased.

You can't hide thinking 'bout me all the
time; my ultimate aim is to
please that girl of mine,

So ... come on over, girl; let's make history,
girl; love is on the way; I'll call
the shots and give you all I got,

If you let me.

The Familiarity of You

Enjoying long walks on the beach,
holding hands and knowing you,

Sitting in our favorite chairs silently reading,
looking at TV answering your questions before it's completed,

Understanding your looks, glances, and thoughts, and welcoming
the thereafter,

Laughing at jokes only we share that no one else understands
or cares about,

Touching and caressing that spot that you know so well and
knowing what to expect and welcoming it,

My G-spot to you is my entire being, because you and only you
know how to turn me on.

Yes, you are my familiarity, and you are turning me on for life.

May-September Affair

Little boy, you hittin' on me; I'm a woman fully grown, and you ain't nothing but a baby.

You look so good—young and sweet—a young, tender roonie lookin'
good enough to eat.

Should I invest in this relationship? I think not or end up in a bed of forget-me-nots.

Lady, age ain't nothing but a number, says he. If that's true, why do me and your mama have so much common?

He just won't leave me alone. Should I take the plunge? What do I
have to lose, or is the relationship too far flung to choose?

I rolled over looking into his face pillow to pillow—and wonder what drama I can expect in this relationship.

Am I just a sexual toy or a future sugar mama? I know not what to;
expect I'll just enjoy this affair with the baby boy and not become faint-hearted.

The relationship ended; we parted as friends, and I truly enjoyed it, so don't pass up the May-September affair; it may all be well worth it.

Let Me Love You

There's warmth between my thighs.

There's life within my womb.

Why don't you want me?

I will wrap myself around you warmly, sweetly, and suck the life seed from you;

Hold it, grow it into the man or woman that will act discreetly.

Why don't you want me?

I will grow old with you, and never tire of you; you are my one ray of hope.

Let me in, I'll be closer than a friend, so

Let me love you!

Telephone Love

I wait for your call each and
Every day in anticipation of
Your telephone call
Of love.

I love your
Sexy word play,

Your phone calls leave
Me weak and panting for more,
But I never miss your calls,
Constantly begging
And panting mi amor.

The ringing of the phone sets me ablaze,
Panties wet,
Hot with sweat,
Can't wait for the next call.

You tease me,
You please me on the phone;
I long to consummate this affair.

You put me off saying let's just talk,
Ooh, how I long for that day.

Your low, sexy voice caresses my soul,
Puts butterflies in my stomach
Uncontrolled.

The day will come when
I will feel the sum of your body and voice in mine,

To   be   fulfilled.

Just for the Love of You

For the love of money, the youths will
sell their bodies and souls.

For the love of fame and notoriety, people will lie,
Plagiarize, and condemn the innocent for gold.

For the love of a commitment from a man or woman
People will perform unscrupulous acts of amour,

For the love of extended life, some would make a bargain
With the devils dejour.

What would you do?

An Unconditional Love

I have loved you all my life even before I knew you,
From the first day I laid eyes on you.

You held me tight both day and night, because yours is
Unconditional love.

My thoughts are with you when I am away, thinking about you
Constantly every day.

When I'm late I panic, afraid of the
consequences, but the trouble
I perceive is only in my mind because
yours is an unconditional love.

I waited for you month after month not sure of your coming,
But when you made your glorious appearance it was all worth
Everything.

You are my sweet bundle of joy—my baby born of my
loins—so cuddly, so small, so loved by me and all.

He is the joy of my life—my baby boy—
he is my unconditional love.

The Essence of You

How do I describe the essence of you?
The aroma you exude after
sex with the early-morning dew.

Your smile as you gaze so beautifully at
the setting sun, sitting side by
side experiencing a one-on-one special moment with you.

Your swaggered walk with just a touch of arrogance and a
backward stare as you walk away.

The dogmatic way you argue with your
friends at who made the best
touchdown of the football game.

The gentle way you play with our children
after work when no one is
looking.

This, my love, is the very essence of you!

When Did You Know You Loved Me?

Did you love me that day you laid eyes
on me in the middle of the
baseball field?

Did you love at the high school dance, dancing cheek to cheek
and stealing kisses under the light of the moon?

When did you know you loved me?

Did you love me in the science lab, while testing an
experiment trying to get a good grade?

Did you love me when you and I parted to different schools,
communicating on holidays and on the phone?

When did you know you loved me?

Did you love me when we were wed in my beautiful white and
you in magnificent black?

Did you love me with the birth of our three kids—all beautiful,
all sweet, all loved with all our fiber?

When did you know you loved me?

Did you love at our seventieth wedding
anniversary surrounded by
friends and family and well-wisher. At that time you
whispered, "I love you," and I knew you loved me all the time.

You Are My Beloved

I see you in the bright sun, with the beams
shining down on you—you
are so beautiful.

The night light of the moon cast a lovely
shadow on your magnificent
form.

I wake up and run to see if you are still
there, my beloved, and would
miss you if you were gone.

In your presence as we cruise the highways
and byways together, I am
confident and strong,

A lovely sight to see with admiring and
envious glances from all.

I love my beloved car!

You Look So Finger-Lickin' Good

I see you looking so sweet as you sashay across the street,
You look so finger-lickin' good,

Sitting high on the stoop with that teeny tiny tee,
You look so finger-lickin' good.

Hey, pretty mama, you going my way?
You look so finger-lickin' good.

Don't look at me sneering that way,
You look so finger-lickin' good.

Those short-shorts are high up your leg-leg,
You look so finger-lickin' good.

Your nonchalant attitude only makes
me want you more each day,
You look so finger-lickin' good.

Go on, go on; I don't care no more; you hurt
my feelings more than you will ever
Know,

But you still

Look
So
Finger-
Lickin'
Good.

71

This is a silly little poem.

Eyes—the Mirror of Your Mind

Eyes so blue, I can see through you.

Eyes so brown, why don't you stick around?

Eyes so gray, I thought I knew you anyway.

Eyes so green, so peaceful and serene.

Eyes so hazel, looking at me with critical appraisal.

Eyes so black, mirror back just what I have or lack.

Love Left Me

Love walked out of my life and left me with
nothing to do; I'm upset, broken-
hearted and confused.

Love walked out early one morning before
the sun came out nice and bright, my
world has been topsy-turvy and turned
my bright, sunny days to night.

I loved them with all my heart and soul,
would lay down my life if I were told.

I walk the streets dejected, unaware of time
or place, wanting to be accepted back
with my lover interlaced.

Love, come on home where you belong and
continue our escapade for lifelong.

I walk the streets day and night looking high
and low for you, and returning home
no ring of the phone leaves me sad and blue.

Love walked out of my life and left me alone
with nothing to do; next time around
I won't be so down; I'll just concentrate on number two.

Close to You

*You've got my head in a haze, and I am walking in a daze
'cause I got to get close to you.*

*The sight of you makes me weak, and it's
hard to compete, with those other guys
trying to make time.*

*You don't know I exist, but I love you more than less
'cause I got to get close to you.*

*Please don't push me away; I promise I won't go astray
'cause I got to get close to you.*

I got to get close to you ... every day.

I got to get close to you ... in every way.

I got to get close to you ... come what may.

*I've got stars in my eyes, and oh how time
flies when I think about you all day
long.*

*My heart skips a beat, and I am dragging my
feet to rush up and say hi, but in the
end it's a bust because I never get the
guts, and I let you just walk on by.*

I just gotta get, gotta get close to you.

Runaway Love

Hey, baby, run on over here; the last time
that I saw you has been over a year.

We parted as friends, but I have been missing
you since then; come on over, love,
and fill this lonely heart again.

I've loved you all my life, I know this for sure;
you have become a part of me, so
open up that door.

True love comes once in a lifetime—maybe
two—and I will never give up on this
love so true.

I miss you, lady, and this I know for sure,
you won't get away, not like you did
before.

So come on over, baby, let's try and start anew, and this
time, pretty baby, we will stick together like glue.

I Love You, Girl

I wake up to the sun shining on your beautiful face, and I think about last night's warm embrace.

Your love is sooo good and sooo very warm, I can't help thinking about your loving arms.

We were intertwined last night in hot sweaty love and lay after like two turtledoves.

I miss you when you are away from me too long and run straight back to you as if you might be gone.

When you look at me my heart flutters with joy; the anticipation of seeing you makes me feel like a schoolboy.

I will love you forever for you are mine all mine; I could never love another because you are too divine.

The Cheating Kind

I saw you with that woman last night sitting on your thigh.

She was looking intently in your face; don't give me no alibi.

*She looked okay but not better than me, but
the way you were looking at her like she
was some cookies.*

*My mother told me you were no good, but my heart was
involved, and I would change you—I thought I could.*

*Daddy said leave that fool, but I could never do that;
for the sake of my children that would be too cruel.*

*I married you 'til death us do part, and death was
upon you when I stabbed you in the heart.*

*I went to jail on a crisp March day and was
put to death on a warm day in May.*

*Listen, my sisters, it's not worth your time to
get involved with the cheating kind.*

The First Time I Made Love

The sun was shining bright, and the leaves were fresh and green on the trees, and I was in love.

His name was Jordan, and he made me feel like a woman fully grown—overabundant and sexually inclined.

His love was good; his love was strong; his love was sweet; it was my very first time making love to a man.

He says he loves me while he makes good love to me, and I like it, because he made love to me for the very first time.

He rubbed my body and kneaded my parts until I screamed and cried for joy; once through, I knew for sure that I would continually come back for more.

My mind was on him both day and night, so hard to get that night out of my mind. For so long I thought I had experienced love, but this time indeed was the very first time.

Years have passed, and occasionally he crosses my mind, and when he does
I will never forget how he made love to me for the very first time.

I Miss You

I miss the long walks and long talks as day's gone, bye.

I miss your smiling face, your warm embrace,
your laughter when the joke is done.

I miss you.

I miss your loving stare, the midnight
dares as love surrounds us.

I miss you.

I miss your happy times, your sad times
as they all melt into one.

I miss you.

You walked out of my life and with that I lost my life and I will

Forever

Miss

You.

Took Me Out

Brought me dinner,

Had me a drink, and

Now you want my

Punanie.

I'm not that easy.

Greasy,

You got a long way to slide.

How Do I Make Love
To My
Self?
With Soft, Warm, Slippery
Fingers

My Sadness Cry

We cry when we are sad and sometimes
cry when we are glad; we even cry
when we are very bad.

It releases the soul and empties in part,
crying cleans and cleanses the broken
heart.

Some fake cry but most are crying for real;
whenever it occurs, it is certainly
a big deal.

Hug the crier, comfort them, assure them
that everything will work out all right;
the day will come, and you may need to
be reassured in this awful plight.

Crying may be underrated or over-abused;
crying wolf one day will make you
see that you are surely on your own for sure.

How underrated, overrated, inebriated
you feel, crying is still a good
release from an awful ordeal.

Jay

I watched you as a little boy so bright,
so intelligent, so full of joy.

You were full of mischief all the while; little
did I know you were a troubled child.

You had to make it on your own, living through
threats and deceit until you were grown.

The family secrets all hid and tucked away,
to finally come out in great display.

Childhood destroyed filled with anger and fear;
if only he knew his relief was so near.

Mother could not know the family disgrace,
trapped in the middle of an offsided embrace.

God will have you when He is ready—no rush, no
push, the road seems steady. Go in peace, my blessed
child, your soul is released, and secrets reviled.

Death Has No Restrictions!

Death is a crossroad that we all must share;
how we leave is an individual affair.

Though rich or poor all share the same fate;
how we're laid to rest will be a family
debate.

Death is indiscriminate, not based on age, sex, race, or
social status; no bribes accepted—we all go nongratis.

Death comes in silence, no alarms or bells. If
your life is not right you will all go to
hell!

For so me death comes with no warning or announcements;
get your life in order; there'll be no time for pronouncements.

When death comes knocking, we could try to run
and cower, but in the end we all must answer.

Your destination is determined by how you live your life in
the end, so live life to the fullest and commit very little sins.

Your road may be rocky; it's all in how you make it. "To
God be the Glory," we all chant and try to commit to it.

Heaven is for some of us without a doubt; you will
only get there by being religiously devout.

I'm Mad

*I'm mad, and I'm not getting over it—not
today, not tomorrow, or next year.*

*You pissed me off without a cause, and
your time is drawing near.*

*Your mama can't save you and your dad either; I'm
gonna get you, and your time is drawing nearer.*

*I didn't do nothing to you, but you messed
with me anyway; now I'm going to
settle this before another day.*

*I hope you are ready for me; to leave no room for
doubt, you ain't leaving here with that ugly pout.*

*So come on, come on and get it over with,
and stop sitting over there; you don't
scare me with that silly little stare.*

*I'm mad, and I don't care who knows; you'd
better watch out before I hit you in the nose.*

Katrina's Destruction

Katrina, Katrina what a destructive display; you ravaged several cities to everyone's dismay.

Nothing could stop you—not tall buildings or other man-made devices—and what was destroyed was a roll of the dices.

Dams busted, streets flooded, death and destruction everywhere, cities destroyed not a brick nor mortar spared anywhere.

People tossed and turned; most were displaced. What lies in their futures is a questionable fate.

Children are missing, whole families are too. Did this city deserve this just due?

Men, women, and children are scattered no place to go, constantly displayed on
every TV show.

Decades of living collapsed in a second; to rebuild will take weeks, months, or years, I reckon.

Life's a battle full of losses and gains, but this life's battle will be hard to regain.

Onward they march with like others hand in hand, mercy granted from the elders
after many desperate demands.

The future is cloudy with little relief in sight; lessons learned, support earned,
leaders scorned not to be contrite.

Escape

Trapped in this lifeless shell, existing on the kindness of strangers that is never there.

Sitting on the edge of this quiescent but crumbling volcano, waiting to erupt.

Feeling as hollow as a carved-out tree hunk empty and barren of life,

Stripped naked to the world laying bare to an uncaring society.

*Barely keeping your head above water, drowning in an ocean of needs, wants, and
desires.*

Slowly being crushed by overwhelming responsibilities of the day-to-day drudgeries of existence.

Eaten alive by insincere plastered-on smiles from emotionally spent individuals.

*Steadily marching onward with heavy-shouldered responsibilities with no relief in
sight.*

In the end relief from this overburdened life game welcome—death.

Sadness Go Away

Ever engulfed in sadness, feeling as if my heart is going to break.

Twisted in this downward spiral of doom, without mercy or relief from this pain.

The shadows surround me, as if covered by a dark, impending veil.

Mercy evades me as if running to catch that dissipating rainbow.

Have mercy on me; loneliness stay away, you pervasive web of fear.

Barren and void of happiness—forever fleeting like snowflakes on a warm face—Lord help rid me of this awful pain I'm feeling and help me out of this apathy. Sadness go away from me and release me from my misery.

Other Poems

The Weighting Game

On another diet, what can I do? Seattle
Sutton, Jenny Craig just to name a few.

It's hard to pick a plan that's right for me;
I've tried them all can't you see?

I like to think that I am a big-boned girl, but
weight increased with time. Who am I fooling?
I'll be two hundred in just a matter of time.

This time its final; there will be no room for doubt,
'cause this is my last diet, this l shout.

Now it's Weight Watchers, and I'm serious this time. The
weighting game is over; I will have no partners in crime.

The weight is coming off; it's about time at last. This
will be the final time or next time I will fast.

The weight is off. I'm skinny now at last; it was
dastardly feat. I can eat what I want, and putting
it back on will be a treat. Ha ha! Ha ha! Ha!

Jimmy

They say the darker the berry the sweeter
the juice, but Jimmy was coffee-o-lay.

He was six feet five and four feet wide;
I'd say he was a man all the way.

He came into my life when I needed him most; no
not shy, just an average guy, no brag nor boast
just fact.

A knight in shining armor, he took care of my needs
with little heed but was a magnificent charmer.

You long for time you cannot have and a life
that cannot return, and in the end, memories
live within that have their turn.

Why cannot those days return and have the life that I
yearn. But if it did, could I ever progress and learn?

Maybe it is not meant to be, and he will
forever live in my memories.

Jimmy ...

Pinky

She's rough around the edges, so her job requires her to be.

She's a woman fully grown, that's what the world can see.

You can call her pinky and most appropriately so,

For that is her signature color, and we have all been told.

Just observe her, and you can see—pink bra, pink barrette,

Pink stockings make it complete.

*She is ultrafeminine and has a pink attitude; arts and crafts are her
value viewed,*

*Good daughter, fair mother; its what's expected of her. Don't
play her cheap; she is gutsy for sure.*

*Miss Pinky—so fair, so bright—keep on keepin' on, all through
the day and night.*

0

Penny Luck

It is said,

"Find a penny, pick it up,
and all day you will have
good luck."

But I say,

"Find a penny, leave it there,
and you'll find someone
who cares."

So, make a decision, and make
it quick, or end up in life love
sick.

We believe in luck; we truly
do, so make your decision
or be done thru and thru.

0

Party

Remember when us was young, and we
twisted and turned our boo-ta on
the dance floor.

Stepping was the way, and we danced the
night away and sweated 'til our
hair went back to the natural way.

We were young, and life was easy-going—
no fuss, no muss the order of
the day was.

Party.
Party.
Party.

Aunt tee tee

*As I look into your face, fine lines and wrinkles grace
your lovely face.*

*Hair is silver. How did the time pass so fast? Why it was
only yesterday that you were out doing that jazz.*

*Your steps have slowed down, but you posture and
spirit is still upright, aging gracefully and beautifully as
time passes by.*

*Nieces and nephews you have by the dozens; we
adore you and implore you don't leave so sudden.*

*Your sisters and most brothers have departed to
Glory, and your seventy-plus years on earth have summoned
many wonderful stories.*

Ugly Thang

Look at him; he looks so fine walking
down the street with that ugly
thang.

They say beauty is in the eye of the
beholder, but what does he see
in her; she so ugly she makes my eyes hurt.

Is she a good cook, or does she make
love oh so fine? I can do all of
that and do it in short time.

How did she get him, lure him into her
web? We both saw him at the
same time, and now they are wed.

He passed me up he did, and I'm as
fine as good wine, to pick her
looking like a cheap shoeshine.

I guess that the way life is, so profound
and out of sorts. It ain't what
you look like; its what's in you heart.

Oprah

Oprah an intelligent, sophisticated Aj 'enu.
They try to bring her down,
but not now; she got something to prove.

She is a well-read woman known throughout the world,
and everyone sits patiently to hear
her final word.

Her generosity is felt by young and old alike,
and her warmth is felt by all
both day and night.

She is a southern gentile lady,
smart and full of grace,
but don't let that fool you because she will get in your face.

Some have challenged her
only to fall in an uncompromising heap.
The children they love her;
she teaches them not to accept defeat.

Oprah, your name rings around the world.
This we all know, and in years to come when we all have
succumb,
her name will prevail multifold.

Family Reunion

We all share a common bond under the sun, by marriage, birth;
no one will be outdone.

The uncles, the aunts, the cousins look! Here they all come, in
trucks, cars, vans, and
SUVs.

Blood ties are what we all share; at least that is what we are
told by our forbearers.

Family reunions are greatly anticipated; this yearly event is
often very complicated.

The gatherings are large with the old, middle-aged and young,
all with the main purpose
to have lots of fun.

The family grows bigger, and so does the reunion; think of the
plans for the next one
makes my head go swooning.

However difficult the plans, no one would be begrudging, the
plans and progress of the
next reunion.

The New Year Promise

2005 went out with a bang, and 2006
brought people in overhanged.

Past promises and vows have long since been
forgotten; new year oaths are soon undertaken.

Forget the past, for that is what it is; new beginnings
and life promises are yours for the taking.

The motherless, fatherless, wifeless, and
husbandless all start anew; with the future at
hand you are bound to make a major coup.

The new year affirms boundless open opportunities; it will
be up to you to take advantage of the endless possibilities.

Start with a positive outlook; forget about past
failures. Only you can make changes by
tasting life's treasures.

So out with the old and in with the new, starting
out fresh has such a wonderful view.

Sleep of Wondrous Sleep

Sleep comes upon me enveloping me in its quiet arms,

Needed rest from the long day's work or play.

*Some accept the welcome slumber; some fight for it unable to
attain the needed rest.*

*Some experience fitful sleep while some sleep like a rock; however,
the sleep attained at the end of the day is not poppycock.*

*While some consider sleep overrated, that may be an individual
belief. It may not be considered as such to the person's sleep
that is aborted.*

*A child sleeping appears so restful and pure; adults fight to go
back to that type of sleep, for it is a special allure.*

Watching the clock, counting time waiting for sleep to dry-dock.

*Relax and wait, it won't be late; sleep will be right on time; it is
an inevitable fate.*

Mandingo Man

Look at the big beautiful Mandingo Man,

Full lips, almond eyes, hair full of tight black curls,

Skin the color of rich black coal,

His eyes as dark as the midnight sky.

This beautiful specimen of a man knocks my soul out of sight.

He is a black Adonis, who could deny.

His voice is of the ages—clear, crisp, mellow, and out of sight.

My love comes down when I see him,
ooowwweee, he looks so damned sweet.

My heart skips a beat as he saunters by; he
is a multitude; I think I'm going to die.

Walk softly by me, Mandingo Man, cause
you are such an eye delight.

Each day makes me feel that I want to take off in flight.

Excitement

Excitement is my name; excitement is my game.

I thrive on it, come alive on it, and can't do without it.

I wake up in the morning looking forward to the day.

*Can't predict it, don't want to miss it, the
adrenaline rush is just what /long for.*

What new adventures await me on my way?

The excitement high is unreal, more than any drug of appeal.

*I get so high that I can reach the sky and come down
in a crash, and it doesn't involve purchases or cash.*

*I get excited on my job and in my play; I get
excited with the joys of life every day.*

Follow my lead; leave the drugs at bay.

You may get excited with life, and, "Have a wonderful day."

Richard, I Miss You Already

He faced his fears, giving us laughter over the years.

His private life was acted out in laughter behind the tears.

*He was a comedian personified, and his humor was always
under a watchful eye.*

*His peers respected and loved him; his admirers felt the
same, and he was whisked away
suddenly after all he overcame.*

*Fame and fortune he did claim, and he was
a reluctant recipient of that anagram.*

*Death came too soon; most would agree
his memory will live on in.infamy*

*Though many deserved awards eluded him, he
plugged right along like a faithful gumshoe.*

*Rest, sweet Richard, your earthly trial is over. Now
celebrate your new ordeal and your new makeover.*

Christmas Cheer

Christmastime a time for cheer.

Santa's elves have worked throughout the year.

*Little children hoping that Santa saw their good
deeds without fear.*

Family and friends leave loads of money at the store's cashier,

*While others feel it's just another holiday
in favor of the profiteers.*

*On Christmas night the kids are all
excited and hold it in revere,*

All hoping to see that special red-nose reindeer appear.

Go to sleep little one, he will soon arrive.

To see him this night may be a dream out of this stratosphere.

I Love Shoes

*Big ones, little ones they are all my weakness; I love them
all. They are my claim to fame and my uniqueness.*

*Imelda Marcos has nothing on me; my
shoes outnumber the fish in the sea.*

*Will I ever have enough? I think not; they
have a favorite spot in my heart,*

*From the lightest light to the darkest black, I
have all colors. Do I have enough—
yes—no, I'll tell you tomorrow.*

*Right now, I'm going shopping, guess what for—
more shoes, more shoes direct me to the store.*

*I bought shoes in England, Spain, and Italy. Are
they all different? Of course, don't be silly.*

*I will go on shopping for more pairs of shoes;
if I don't, I will surely suffer from
shoes blues.*

Shopping Addiction

Shopping is my addiction. I love the
sights and smells of the stores.

Walgreen's to Wal-Mart and Bloomingdales
to Payless, there is no difference
when I want to shop unless I want to
play it safe or dress for success.

The Dollar Store is the place to be, more
bargains than I could imagine to see.

The beautiful clothes, the beautiful shoes, the
beautiful furniture is a draw to me,
I love being in the mix of shopping, can't you see?

Ordering online, in the catalogs, or in the store,
shopping from all sites is not at all a bore.

Shopping is my addiction of choice, causing
no harm or pain to me or others, but
when I shop, clear out my way unless you are a jogger.

One day my shopping trend will end, and
that will be a disaster, but until then
will shop like a drill master.

Sleepwalker

Sleepy head, sleepy head walking around in a daze.
How she drives her car we are all amazed.

She's tired when she wakes up and when she goes to bed;
what she does in between would make us all afraid.

Her eyes are droopy, and her demeanor is too; she
makes it through the day with a limited view.

Her husband says she's just sleepy, and her kids
just want her to wake up; the neighbors look for
her day and night if she would just stay up.

Riding the trains every day, she is in a deep
coma; the conductor doesn't know where she
gets off. She might ride to Tacoma.

Let her sleep, she needs her rest; when she
willfully wakes up is anyone's guess.

Good Old Nurses

Oooooowwwweeeee, I'm so tired, tired as it can be.
Walking these halls long ago was nothing for me.

My legs hurt, and my feet are swollen, and my back is
aching too, I'm just so tired I don't know what to do.

It seems like yesterday when I was young and energetic,
ran down halls for any bell—that was my objective.

Now I'm old, or so it seems that way, and my
youthful get-up-and-go was gone yesterday.

I see young nurses come and go. Old nurses stay and stay.
Maybe the young nurses have gone to find a better way.

Nursing is an honorable profession—hard
word and diligence is a good perception.

So wait, give it a second chance; nurses
and nursing is the ultimate plan.

Mister Cool

Look how he glides down the street. Mr.
Cool is so cool he can't be beat.

He is sharp as a tack, and no one would argue—
silk suits, wingtip kicks you can't beat or follow.

He strolls through the neighborhood taking in the scene.
He's a man on a mission; no one could break his routine.

White teeth shinning against that so-tan skin,
looks like Clark Gable to our chagrin.

His manner is captivating, attitude devastating; his
allure is addictive, to the point of revelating.

The ladies all love him; they think he's so
fine. He'll break your heart without thinking
your complete will he has to define.

The men all jealously respect him; he is no punk. Smith and
Wesson is at his side; risk it, and he will use it just for fun.

Car is a Caddy, won't have it any other way. A
man of his caliber would never stray away.

Look in your local neighborhoods; I am sure you
all have one. he's easy to spot—can't mistake
him for a jock, for some they've just begun.

Badonk-a-donk Butt

There goes that girl with the badonk-a-donk butt; looks
like she got two potato sacks riding on her butt.

Badonk-a-donk butts can be big, and it can be
small; they usually have hardly no shape at all.

They come in all colors, shapes, and sizes, to see
one is to know one right before your very eyes.

They look like they smell and probable do; check
yours in the mirror, you might have one too.

Pretty girls have them and ugly girls too; there
is no segregation, come on get a clue.

These kinds of butts have been around from the
beginning of time. Identification and demonstration
can sometimes make you go blind.

So, fellas, beware, and take care of your
eyes, the badonk-a-donk butt
has been known to take lives.

Talking Chatty Cathy

Chatty Cathy won't let nothing in; Chatty Cathy
she talks and talks again and again.

She talks so much she talks all day; she
works a lot and earns her pay.

She talks in her sleep I do believe. Will she
ever stop talking No! don't be so naïve.

She was quiet one time, scared me to death,
only to find out she was out of breath.

Will she ever get laryngitis, she'd talk
right through it and get tonsillitis.

Talk, talk, talk. That's what she do all day.
Talk, talk, talk, and you are bound to
get a replay,

All over again!

Nevoida

Chocolate Jones

Oh, sweet choocoolaate is my demise, dark
chocolate, brown chocolate, even white.

I love the taste upon my lips—so sweet,
so smooth, so bad for my hips.

It comes in bars, stars, and tiny little tidbits,
anyway it comes it can enter my lips.

I say, oh no, not chocolate today for a
chocolate fast is the order of the day.

How long will it last? Five, four, three, two, one
minute, for the addiction is strong, and willpower
is weak, and I'm not willing to defend it.

Snickers is the bar of choice; I dream of the
bar entering my mouth. Oh, sweet bar of truth,
release me from this never-ending ruse.

Oh, well. Oh, well, I've lost the battle and won't fight the
feeling; succumb to the bar, and set my taste buds reeling.

Sophisticated Lady

*Sophisticated lady, that's what you are, full
of style, grace, and savoir faire.*

*Well educated, intoxicating yet submissive to her man, her
life is a testament, and her man's heart is her ultimate plan.*

*She's a spiritual woman and praises God with
every living breath; her children love her and
are encouraged with each and every step.*

*Her embodiment is superior, but she is a down-
home girl; stand near her and hear her,
and she'll give your world a whirl.*

*She has jet-black hair with soft brown eyes that
will be perfect for all times; she would argue the
point, but it's clear to see she is a lady refined.*

*Take care of this woman—a modern-day saint—
soft eyes, soft thighs, her husband maintains.*

Tootsie

Black Girl

Black girl, black girl, why are you so scorned? Full lips and
full hips, imitated never duplicated; ours was self-born.

She walks down the street full of style and grace,
you would never know she is living day to day.

She can squeeze blood from a turnip; she
proves this every day, and you could learn
lessons from her to the world's dismay.

Black man stand by her side, this a perfect match, put all
your pride aside; you know she is your perfect catch.

Colors ranging from fair to dark black, coming in all shapes
and sizes—a variety pack—take your choice; you will
surely voice I will keep her foremost and never look back.

She has a temper, but you can get over that; just rub her
shoulder, reassure her and that together we can combat.

Take her; she's a jewel you won't live to regret it, or
suffer the consequences of absence and soon forget.

My Son

I am so proud you are my seed; I gave you life in its entirety, and my responsibility to you I accept wholeheartedly.

I will teach you to be a man, for that is my duty, and the world will not judge you for lack of ingenuity.

In the dawn of my waning years, I hope by example that my legacy will live on and won't be trampled.

In this difficult world we live in, growing up a man is hard, but with guidance he can be equipped with the proper guards:

Love,
Respect,
Dignity,
Education, and
Determination

This new man—my seed—will be equipped with the knowledge a man needs to carry on the legacy instilled in him to succeed.

A Love Poem to My Granddaughters

Here you are presented to me, such a small and beautiful bundle of joy.
I watched you grow inside her tummy and wished you were a girl not a boy.

I dressed you in pretty pink dresses looking oh so sweet; you spilled your favorite ice cream—"Choocoolate Fudges"—onto the street.

I wiped the tears that were spilling, kiss-kiss, hug-hug for life; I will fondly remember this day until the afterlife.

I whisper sweet nothings in your ear and sing you lullabies as you sit near, wishing this would last forever and a day or until her way is perfectly clear.

I love you with all my heart and soul, a replica of my daughter to behold.

The Country Preacher
Bishop Jordon

A country preacher is what he calls himself, but he is the ambassador of spiritual truth and wisdom.

From humble beginnings he came and never forgot his place, giving back to the community is his state of grace.

A family man is he, but also a husband, father, grandfather, friend, and counselor to his entire congregation.

Busy in meeting and counseling people far and wide, giving spiritual advice, to save the souls of all is his only cry.

Bountiful and blessed congregation to be able to listen to the sound of his voice, he
is a teacher and preacher; God gave him no other choice.

A passionate and God-filled man is his claim to fame, and his generosity is well known throughout the land.

St. Mark loves you, I think all will agree, and would be hard pressed to find someone to disagree.

Take it slow, good Reverend, this church is your personal affair; all who don't take
heed to your spiritual faith teaching will need to answer in prayer, prayer, prayer.

Puerto Rican Girl

Purebred Puerto Rican girl, hair wild and full of curls,

You can't tell her nothing; look how she struts her strut;
tangle with her, and you will get kicked in the butt.

You could say she has an attitude, but that's not fair; with
her modus operandi, you should approach with strict care.

She is a hot-blooded woman; they are well known for
that; cross her, and you will have no questions just fact.

When she salsas, men drop dead in their tracks.
It's understandable 'cause she's got it like that.

Family ties are special and precious to her—not
neglectful, not fretful—these are the ties she prefers,

Handle with care this precious jewel; not everyone
understands her, but that is not the majority's rule.

Bruce the Barber

My barber/beautician so smooth and debonair,
he coifs my hair with immaculate flair.

He cuts and styles with such expert grace, when
you walk out you walk with a royal face.

Brown-skinned man with beauty from the motherland, as I
watch him style each and everyone's hair strand by strand.

He is immaculate in his appearance, won't have it any other
way, and oh so distinguished with those little sparks of gray.

One hundred percent man that's what he is, and
if you doubt it, he will give you the biz.

Cool, calm, and collective that is his manner; he
is a gentleman, and he wears it like a banner.

Men, women, and children, he treats them all the same,
and all keep coming back to get that hair tamed.

Jazz Man

I listen to the melodious sounds from your instrument
as you play your heart away, head bobbing keeping
in time with the rhythm me thinks that's okay.

Sitting in my chair eyes closed letting the music flow over my
mind, knowing the end will come; it's just a matter of time.

Beautiful jazz man your sounds are so mellow and smooth,

How do you come up with the tunes, Mr. Jazz
Man so sexy, so sensuous, and so cool.

The talent you are blessed with puts everyone in a better
mood; keep on playing, it's not just another tune.

Soft music titillating and uplifting you when you are
feeling low, and helps you stay up and wanting to go.

Keep playing the tunes, Mr. Jazz Man, the
world loves you—you and your band.

I Love You, Daddy

You are so big and strong as I see you
walking down the street,

Demanding respect of the community and friends you meet.

As your daughters we loved you and waited every
day, and Mr. Jones always got his way.

Your discipline was strict and punishment swift,
and the love thereafter just as quick.

Your work was hard, and you never complained,
responsibility staunch but you remained the same.

Steadfast love for your family, you did it all—
deacon, father, husband, and friend in a brawl.

The day of your death I cried like a baby but felt in
retrospect your responsibilities were now heavenly.

My love everlasting no one can replace; I
love you, Daddy, forever and a day.

Dear Mama

*You have been the one bright spot in my life even after
death; I miss you most when I am quiet thinking to myself.*

*The three of us were always too beautiful in your eyes,
nothing ugly about us impaired your eyesight.*

*My spirits are lifted when I think of your unconditional
love for me, and my mind is at rest with that decree.*

*So pretty to look at—tall, elegant, and queenly,
blazing light eyes looking soulful and serene.*

*Singing church songs by day and night, so
beautiful the melody I could listen for life.*

*God took her with Him to my dismay; I now have a
beautiful angel watching over me forever and a day.*

*I miss her, I miss her so much my heart is broken in two,
but I know she is in good hands with the Father so true.*

Peace Be Still

*I sit and stare and sit in my place; it's hard
to determine how long I must wait.*

*Time passes so slowly when you are watching
the clock—can't rush it, can't adjust
it, can't make it start or stop.*

*In Jamaica they say everything is IRE, the
Bahamians it is slow down MON; holding to
their advice would be a good plan.*

*It's so hard to remain in place, when all signs
point to you getting back in the rat race.*

*"Slow and steady wins the race," at least that's what they
all say, but the waiting is hard, and it's difficult to stay.*

*Hold fast and steady—good things come to those who wait—
and in the end you will win many rewards at an alarming rate.*

So Easy and So Cheap

Slow and easy is the way, can't rush her,
can't push her to our dismay.

Can't put a fire up under her butt; if you
try, she'll just ask, what! what!

She acts really tired most of the time, and sooo
damned cheap she won't spend a single dime.

She will hunt you down for a quarter; don't pay her
back you might as well walk on live mortar.

She is a slow skinflint in the worst kind of way—
money in her hands lasts forever and a day.

She's just like her daddy, that's what they all say,
and nothing you can do can make her sway.

Little, short, cheap thing that is her claim to fame; she
wants to win the lotto but too cheap to play the game.

Val

Displaced African Queen

*There she goes walking so cool and tall; she's
really from Africa, maybe Senegal.*

*Her skin of dark chocolate so whipped and
refined, and don't try to replace her or
you will find yourself reassigned.*

*She can match wits with the best of them, we know that for a
fact; just ask the casualties when she read them the riot act.*

*She's fully ambitious and will give it her all; study
holds her back; she's pulling a stone wall.*

*Watch her, she's feisty and will get all she's due; in the
meantime, in between time, we'll see what she'll do.*

To my friend Jem

Closet Fast Girl

They think they know her, but they don't, while
she sits wondering what the hell they want.

They walk past her desk with their smug attitudes, but
if they mess with her, she can show them a mood.

She knows all the latest tunes to the surprise of many;
don't play her cheap even though she looks primly.

Her manner is calm, but inside she's seething, she won't
let the world know that she is outwardly acting.

She is the Closet Fast Girl, and this we know, but one
day, one day the whole world will be her bistro.

To my friend Ro

Crazy Girl Friend

*Crazy girl, crazy girl, what you talking about? I
don't know what next is coming out yo mouth.*

*She'll talk about the news as if she were a scholar,
but you paid for that info for only a dollar.*

*When she reads a book, it takes her five years; the
next addition is out, and she don't know it's here.*

*You can't contradict her on any subject; she
will argue with you about the objective.*

*Come on, crazy girl, give us a break; we are
all sitting here getting a headache.*

*Don't change what you're doing; we love you
all the same, but sometimes you give
us nightmares with your constant refrains.*

To my friend Lo Lo

Pretty Brown Horse Man

*I see you riding your horse so big and
tall, with very little effort at all.*

*You look so fine in your chaps and gear, I find
myself getting weak when you are near.*

*On that horse you are an Egyptian God, and
back on earth you still have that elegant.*

*My eyes light up when they fall upon you, and my
soul erupts like taking a sip of home brew.*

*Hearing your voice makes my head start swimming, and
I break out in a cold sweat hearing birds busy singing.*

*Let me in to your life, pretty brown horse man,
and include me in your game plan.*

*Please don't hesitate although good things
come to those who wait. If you look
hard and try, I could be your soul mate.*

*So let's get started; time is clicking ticktock. I want
to come over and unlock your magic clock.*

Unbelievable Drama Queen

I saw her waving her arms vigorously in the air,
animated expressions of frank despair.

She turn tears on and off as if it were water, and if you
don't believe her, she'll turn you into antimatter.

Her drama is well known far and wide. Who
does she think she's fooling with that
jive?

She wakes in the morning with her schemes in full plan and
will carry out her efforts unless she has a vigilant man.

He keeps her attitude in tow, which is a hard thing to
do, but his duty is to make sure she gets her just dues.

His rewards will be heaven, this we all know,
but until then my brother just take it
real slow.

Jeannie

Big-Boneded Baby

Big-boneded baby standing with your hand on your hip, catching everyone's eye, but she ain't gonna trip.

She walks with confidence, and that ain't no joke, and she will get you told with a single word stroke.

The guys all swoon when she enters the room; the girls all playa hate and start to fume.

The girl is heavy but not in weight, and has no problems getting a date.

*Her IQ is genius—she's no dumb blonde—and her portfolio is heavy with
bearer bonds.*

Be careful how you handle her for she is the queen of her throne; she is not one to play with, or you will experience the frigid zone.

Hear ye, hear ye, come one come all; learning her life experiences will be a ball.

To My Daughter

How do I love thee? Well, let me see.

I've loved you since God blessed me with pregnancy.

I carried you for nine months, love ever growing for you.

Brought you into this cold, cruel world, and let no harm come to you.

You are my blessing until the day I die. No one can replace this love I have inside.

*You are my daughter, a blessing from God; without hesitation I say this from
my heart.*

Sha'Quaan

Hey, Sha'Quaan, why act so rude, eyes a blazing she ain't no prude.

She talks a good game and would put most to shame.

Walking and swinging that pony, we all know that it's phony.

Sha'Quaan, Sha'Quaan, don't be so mean, or what you want is to cause a scene.

*Her kids call her mama; she won't answer to that. Her husband feels fully disgusted
and trapped.*

*She is styling and profiling on guard at all times. Sha'Quaan, calm down before
someone drops a dime.*

Big hoop earrings hanging from her ears, walking confidently without fear.

*Her days are numbered as sure as you know, but until then her main thought is to
go, go, go.*

To my friend Theresa

Big Ole Fat Girl

Hey, fat girl, where you been? Walking down the street ice cream dripping from
your double chin.

Up every day at the crack of dawn going over the menu plan, trying to decide
whether to cook in a pot or a frying pan.

You'd better stay out of her way or be scorned, because the dress she has on is on the verge of being torn.

Hey, fat girl, don't you care about that roll around your waist, or is your immediate
concern the pasta on your plate?

The kids all tease her, say she looks like Fat Albert. They had better watch out, their
life is in hazard.

Diet plan after diet plan, they never seem to work. Is it some skinny girl's plan to
drive you from beef to pork?

Hey, fat girl, stop stressin' about your size. Your husband and children don't care
how big your thighs.

About the Author

I am a nurse who has been in my profession for over forty years; suddenly poems started forming in my head, and I decided to write them down. Once doing this I shared some of my works with my coworkers, who told me that they were good and that I should get them published, so here they are. Hope that everyone likes what they read and and can connect with them.

About the Book

These poems where floating around in my head, and I started to write them down and wanted to share them with people to determine if they felt they were as good as I feel they are. They are divided into four sections. They range from sad to thought-provoking prose. I think that you can read some of these and find a kinship with some of them at different times of your life.